GHOSTS

HOSTS

True Ghost Stories

SUE BAUMGARDNER

Other Sue Baumgardner books

Non-fiction
Disabled?
10 Basic Steps To Take Back Your Life

Fiction
Out Of The Darkness

Middle Grade Readers
Jean Alfred's New Home

He Would Not Forget, Not Ever

GHOSTS HOSTS
True Ghost Stories
By Sue Baumgardner

First Amazon Edition March 2017

For my husband, R. Mike Baumgardner who has encouraged me to believe in my ghosts and their presentments.

For my daughter Emily, who shares a close relationship between the next dimension and this, with me.

FOREWARD:

I believe most of us can agree that a ghost is the presence of a spirit who does not live in our earthly realm and does not occupy a vessel of flesh and blood. Sometimes, they appear to inhabit a flesh and blood body and other times, they make their presence known without any physical appearance, and then sometimes they appear only in part or in a hazy appearance.

In most of the ghost stories presented here, I have used the ghosts who have visited me in my sleep. Dreams, you say, just dreams. Yes, that is what I struggled with for many years. However, I have come to realize they are real and actual visits from real and actual spirits. It is my hope that the reader, believer or not, can gain some entertainment and perception from my (true) ghosts stories.

By the way, my favorite ghost is the Holy Ghost!

HUGHIE NIGHTMARES

All too soon, the nightmares began, and through them, I came to understand that my beloved grandfather had passed from this world.

One month before my fourth birthday, I lost the one person most precious to me. Hughie, my step-grandfather slipped away from us in surgery for a kinked bowel. No one told me that he was gone and not coming back. It took a while for me to figure it out. The whispers behind closed doors had me too frightened to ask what was going on.

While he did 'visit' me in those dreams, it was never pleasant. We constantly ran from bad-guys. We ran through long, winding passages and dark places. Hughie knew where we were running to while the bad guys were at a slight disadvantage, not being familiar with the territory where we led them.

The dream varied some, but always followed the same frightening plot. This saga continued to haunt me over and over again until I was in puberty. At this time, I finally shared my nightmare with my mother. "Oh Susanne," she exclaimed. "Hughie needs your prayers. That's why he keeps coming to you. He is trying to show you his need. He is in purgatory and needs your prayers to carry him to Heaven." She told me this in an excited whisper. It was a sacred moment. Instinctively, I knew she was right. That very day, I began to pray for my dearest Hughie. From that day to this, I continue to pray for him every day and I have never had another of those 'visits' from Hughie.

*

OLE' GRAMMIE

At eleven years old, I stood in the funeral parlor over the casket of my great-grandmother Anna. She looked like she was just sleeping. I felt no sadness, no remorse; I felt nothing. She was a lovely lady whom I admired but had pretty much taken for granted for all of my life. I saw her often as she lived with my grandmother, Nanny. Nanny was vivacious and I loved her dearly. To me, Ole' Grammie was just her ancient mother ~ nothing too important to me or my daily life. She spent most of her time sitting by the window, reading her bible. Occasionally, she stood and filled her little watering can and watered her African Violets, or took a few pills. And I watched her take out her teeth to brush them every night before she stole away to bed, before dark in the summer time.

When I was probably about four years old, she caught me pulling on my teeth one day. "Can't you get them out?"

"No," I answered.

"Pull harder," she advised. "Look. Place your fingers here." She showed me how to do it. Still, I had no luck. That is the one time I remember any real interaction between the two of us. Yet as I left the funeral parlor, my aunt came up behind me and put her hands on my shoulders.

"Come on Sue; let's go for a little walk."

That's when I realized that my whole body was trembling, though I had no idea why. I remember walking down the sidewalk with my aunt but I don't remember our conversation. I do recall, however, how I loved her for being concerned with my wellbeing.

How long it took, I'm not sure. Sometime thereafter, I'd guess within a few months, 'Ole Grammie's nightly visits began. I woke to go to the bathroom. I looked over toward my bedroom door and she stood there in my doorway. As I looked at her, she started to walk towards me. I closed my eyes. When I opened them again, she stood where she had been when I closed them, and she then proceeded to walk closer. I was terrorized! But I KNEW this could not be real. She was DEAD! (Unlike the Hughie visits, Ole' Grammie's visits were not spread out over days or weeks. Her visits were nightly.)

I decided to prove to myself that this was not real. I left my bedroom lamp on, beside my bed, confident in my plan. I opened my eyes hours later, and there she stood, in my doorway. She began her slow walk towards my bed. I reached up and place two fingers on the lightbulb of my lit lamp. OUCH!

Squeezing my eyes shut, I eventually found sleep again, knowing that it was all a horrible dream. Hours later, I awoke to a bright sunny morning. First thing, I pulled my hand from beneath my pillow and held it up in front of my face. Before me, I beheld two fingers scorched white and blistered.

At fifteen years old, as I stepped into adulthood, I finally opened up and shared this terrifying ritual with my mother.

"Ole' Grammie would never frighten you like this. I'm sure of that. She was a gentle, loving soul. No, she would never do this. I can assure you, that is not her that you are seeing. Perhaps some evil force is torturing you. But now that he has been found out, with you telling me, I doubt if he will bother you anymore."

Whether my mother was wise in these matters, or I simply believed and made it so, is up to debate. The fact remains that I never saw Ole' Grammie again. It was a great relief to wake in the night, look up at my doorway, throw back the covers, and go pee!

MOM

It was about this time that my mother told me about her experience with her Grampy Bert. My baby brother, Tommy, had died the same day he was born. It seems that Mom had contracted the German measles, without realizing it, while she carried him. The measles, the doctor told her, had all gone in to the baby and totally messed him up. His inner organs were in a non-functional quagmire. Mom blamed herself for her child's death. Because the doctor said to her, "Why didn't you tell me you had the measles," she mistakenly deduced that if she had told the doctor of her rash, he could have done something and saved the baby.

Two years later, my mother gave birth to a baby girl, and thirteen months later, another baby girl. Now caring for four young children (my older brother, myself, and my two young sisters) along with carrying all that guilt for the death of her Tommy, my mother's nerves went to pieces. She admittedly wallowed in guilt and self-pity.

One day, as she sat reclined in the Morris Chair, which had been handed down from Ole' Grammie and Grampie Bert, she was especially despondent. As she wept, Grampie Bert stepped into the room and walked over to her. He knelt beside her and took her hand. He apparently talked some good sense into her and she was filled with renewed courage. All too soon, he stood and drew his hand from hers, resting on the arm of the Morris Chair. She clutched his hand, "Oh Grampie, don't leave me so soon!"

"I have to, Vi. It's time for me to go." As he drew is hand from beneath hers, he evaporated into thin air. (Grampie Burt had died eight years prior to this.)

ME

A large, olive skinned, black headed woman, dressed in black taffeta and nylon stockings, stood by my bed. I was miserably ill with pneumonia. Yet she did not mention my sickness, or even the fact that I was in bed. She rambled on and on about nothing that interested me; I tried to be patient. I tried to stay awake and not appear rude and fall to sleep while she talked to me. Half way through a sentence, with one hand extended in an explanation of some sort and her mouth open, she melted into the wall as a man dressed in a business suit and gray fedora appeared.

I knew this was impossible. I must have missed something - misinterpreted what actually had just happened. The man was pleasant enough, but as he spoke, several other people appeared at my bedside.

I began to cry. Knowing I had lost my mind, I cried myself to sleep.

After the fever broke, I decided that it must have been the codeine in the prescription cough syrup that I had taken. Perhaps I was actually allergic to codeine? Surely those had been hallucinations.

*

Pneumonia became a winterly thing for me. I came down with it at least once every winter ~ either the week before or the week after Christmas.

Several years after the above visitors, I again laid in my bed, stricken with pneumonia, propped up on pillows. As I rested between coughing spasms, I heard and felt my cat, Sammy, jump up on my bed, at my feet. He walked up the bed beside me and dragged his tail across my hand as he approached my pillow. Sam took his place curled around the top of my head. While I was comforted with his warm presence, I did worry that his fur might bother me in my condition.

I fell to sleep. I don't know for how long, but when I awoke, with Sam still curled around my head, I could tell that my fever had broken and I was on the mend, though still very much in a weakened condition. I felt Sammy stand and jump from my bed. I heard his feet hit the hardwood floor. And he was gone ~ back where ever he lives in the beyond. You see, a few years before this bout of pneumonia, we had buried Sammy up behind the garden.

*

That beastly pneumonia came back again the next winter, right after Christmas. This time, I lie on the living room couch, propped up on pillows again, to slow the coughing. My husband had gone to work, early that morning and my children were in school. I was home alone. As I awoke from a nap, I heard the trash truck roll up the street. "On no," I thought. I had asked my husband to put out the trash, before he went to work. Normally, this was my job, but I was too sick this day. We had a lot of trash from Christmas. I was afraid he had not put it out and now we would have a garage full of trash by next week. Very weak, I raised my head from the pillows and looked out into the garage. The trash cans were gone! Wonder of wonders ~ my husband had remembered to put it out. Thank goodness. I fell back to sleep.

Later that afternoon, I awoke again, with my fever broken. I smiled, gratified that I knew I was getting better and ... my hubby had put out the trash for me. That was such a relief ... Then it struck me: I had looked through the living room wall and into the garage and seen the trash cans! "Impossible!" I dragged myself up, walked into the kitchen and opened the door to the garage. I looked down to the front garage door. There stood the trash cans, not in their usual place, but right where I had seen them from the couch, on the other side of the wall!

Now I know this wasn't a ghost sighting. But it's almost like I was the ghost! Do we have a third eye? HOW DID I SEE THROUGH THAT WALL???

DAD

My Dad did not believe in spirits visiting the earthly
realms. Not only did he not believe in it, he forbade us
to talk about such things. Well that is, he forbade us to
until the day he told us about his experience.

Dad woke up, next to Mom, one night. Their bed was
shaking violently. "Vi," he said. "Why are you shaking
the bed?" Mom did not answer. She was deep in sleep.
He looked around; nothing else in the room was
shaking.

The bed continued to shake for several minutes.

After that, Dad believed.

EMILY

Emily was the shy one in our family. But my cousin, Leo, could always bring her out of her shell. When Leo came to visit, Emily brought him her ukulele. Leo played her ukulele and sang love songs to her which he made up as he went along. Four year old Emily stood at his knee with her head bowed. When he stopped, she asked for more, and more he gave her. They had a special rapport.

One afternoon, as Emily sat at the kitchen table eating a snack, I told her, "Emy, Mama is going to run down to the store. Dad is downstairs watching TV. I'll be right back." The store was only about a half mile away and I did return within minutes. As I walked through the kitchen door, I was startled by the look on Emily's face. Still sitting at the kitchen table, she looked up into my eyes. I swear she looked gray. "Emy, what is it?" I rushed over to her.

Her little eyes were open wide as a spooked cat.
"Mama, I saw Leo."
"While I was gone?"
"Yes, Mama. He came in front of the refrigerator. It was only his head and top and he wore a white hood and he was smiling."
This seemed very odd but my main concern was in reassuring my little girl. Nothing I said, however

reassured her ~ Until, that is, my grandmother called us a couple of hours later.

"Sue," she said, "Leo died today."

Now I understood, and so did little Emily. It was the kindest thing Leo could have possibly done for that little girl who loved him so dearly. She was happy that he chose her to visit on his way out of this world. He had somehow reassured her that all was well, as I never could have.

*As a side note: Emily's ukulele disappeared with Leo's death. We searched the house over but never found it.

*

Fast forward about a dozen years and my grandmother, Nanny passed away. Nanny and I had always been close. My daughter Emily and Nanny were also very close. Within weeks after Nanny died, she came to Emily in a dream. Emily knew she was in her bed sleeping as Nanny entered. Emily also knew that my deceased grandfather, who died before I was ever born, waited for Nanny out in the hall.

Emily hugged Nanny and told her how happy she was to see her. She said she never expected to see her after she died. "You've got to go see Muzey too," she exclaimed. "She will be so happy to see you, Nanny!"

"No, no, I'm not going to see her yet. I will eventually, but not yet."

"But why not, Nanny? She would be so happy!"

"Well," Nanny told her, "I'm still a little put out with her right now."

"Why," Emily asked.

"Oh, it's the newspaper thing."

That's all Nanny told her about it, during their visit.

Later that day, Emily and I went down to Muzey's (my mother) and told her about Emily's dream. "Oh dear," my mother lamented.

"Do you know what she was talking about, Muzey?"

"I do. Nanny wrote out her own obituary years ago. She knew what she wanted printed about her life. She gave it to me for safe keeping. I put it in the safe. But when I went to the safe after she died, I couldn't find it. So, I had to write what I could remember. I know it was not what Nan wanted."

"Huh," Emily said. "You know it was strange. I didn't see it as strange in the dream, but after I woke up, I thought it was strange; Nanny had no eyes. It was just black and blank where her eyes should have been."

My mother's hand flew to her lips as she gasped. "Oh Emily!" She cried. It seems that the hospital called Mom in the night, when Nanny passed and told her. The doctor asked Mom if they could have Nanny's eyes. Mom told them she couldn't give them permission until she talked with her only sibling, her brother. "Mrs. Thibodeau," the doctor said, "We don't have time, I'm afraid. I have ten minutes before it will be useless. My mother granted him permission, but told no one! She was worried that her brother might be upset with her, so she decided to keep it secret.

Do you need any more proof that these nightly visits can be for real?

*

Izaiah is Emily's oldest son. His father, Jeff, died when he was just a baby. When he was three, his mother married his step-father (and adoptive father) Michael. The week of the wedding, Izaiah's first father came to Emily in a dream. He told her that he was pleased she was marrying Michael. "He will be a great father to my son."

I did not know this until Emily told me, after I told her of my dream. I dreamed that I was on a lake, standing on a dock and Jeff came walking up the dock towards me. I had never met him, but as he approached me, I knew him. I knew his genuine caring for Izaiah. "I will always watch out for him, from where I am. He's going to be fine."

MY DREAMS

Having just mentioned my Jeff dream, this seems a good time to get into more of my dreams.
Having been brought up in the Roman Catholic Church, divorce was a big 'no-no' for me. However, I did divorce after 24 years of marriage. Yes, I divorced and I remarried. Understanding the rules, I stayed away from the 'Communion Rail.' I remember attending Mass and weeping in my pew as others walked down to receive Holy Communion. This went on for several years before I received an annulment.

I dreamed that my husband and I drove into the old Grenci & Ellis building in Frankfort (which is no longer there) late at night. Our battery had run down and we needed someone to give us a boost. (My Dad had worked there when I was very young, so I was familiar with the place.) We walked down towards the Prospect end of the (huge) building in hopes to find someone working nights who could help us. At one point, I told my husband to go on without me. I went back to a barn which was out front, mid-way of the building. (Not really, but in my dream.) As I approached the closed double barn doors, I sensed there was an evil presence inside. But I knew my faith, my love of the Lord would support me. I knew I had to enter the barn.

As I opened the doors, I was sucked inside by a violent wind. The wind threw me around the barn, from one wall to the next. I knew I had osteoporosis and this was dangerous because the doctor had told me that my bones were like glass. However, I knew that the Lord would support me. I was not afraid. Over and over again, I was blown, thrown around the walls of that old barn! At long last, the wind died and I fell about ten feet down to the floor, unharmed.

I stood and walked out of the barn. Heading back down a dusty path through the weeds, I walked towards where I had left my husband. I came upon a young boy riding a donkey. I expected to speak to the boy, but this did not happen. They stopped right in front of me and the donkey communicated with me through thought only. He thanked me for the fight I had just endured. He explained that it had not only freed me, but it had freed him and the boy also.
I knew my sins were forgiven and that I was free to receive my Lord.

Next morning, I got up and went to Sunday Mass. When the others proceeded down to the Communion Rail, I did not weep. I joined them.

*

Living in Waterville for fourteen years, I enjoyed many close friends. One of the very closest was my next door neighbor, Naji. She was a first generation Lebanese American. What a lady! She taught me a lot about cooking, home making, business entrepreneurship, and life in general. After I moved away, we stayed in touch. Although we didn't see each other often, we usually touched bases about once a year.

As it neared Easter, I fixed a little basket and drove to Naji's house with it. No one was home, so I left it with a note, inside her storm door. I waited for months for her to call, but never heard from her. I finally called her daughter-in-law to see if Naji was okay. She said Naji had passed away about a year ago. I was pretty sad to think that I didn't get to say goodbye.

A few nights later, I sat in a luxurious bath. The tub was more of a pool ~ a large soft textured, perhaps marble, pool ~ in which I sat with the water just above my breast. A light fog, or steam, rose from the water all around me. As I gazed in front of me, Naji appeared out of the fog. She too sat breast high in the water, smiling. "Naji," I exclaimed. Without effort, she appeared closer, directly in front of me.

"I knew you would see me, Sue. Most people wouldn't, but I knew you would."

"Oh Naji, I thought I'd never see you again. Are you happy?"

"Oh yes Sue! We all are! We are so happy you cannot believe it! And close to you. Sue we are so close! We are right next to you! Most people will never realize that, but I know you will believe me."

We embraced and had a lovely reunion that night. I woke up so terribly happy. I still had not told her goodbye. No need. It's never goodbye. Though I don't believe I've ever seen Naji in another dream, I know she's close and will be waiting for me when I make the crossing.

*

My Dad's death was the most difficult death I've ever experienced. Probably for more than one reason: 1) Because I loved and respected him so deeply and 2) Because he suffered so for the last five weeks of his life, while my sister and I took shifts in staying with him at the hospital and attempting to meet his every need. We watched him float between this world and the next. He called us his angels. It broke our hearts when he finally refused any more breathing assistance. But we know that now, he truly is with the angels.

I will now post some journal entries I kept of dreams, in the last two years before Dad died:
July 1, 2011
Two night ago, I dreamed Mike and I were swimming in a very large pool. Dad was there too. Sometimes he pulled on my foot as he swam below me – just kidding around. Mike and I were trying to fill an old-time urn – water vessel – like they used in Jesus' time. After we got it filled, I said, "Now how are we toing to get this out of here?" I figured that in lifting it up and out over the side of pool – we would sink and drown! But when we had it to the edge, Vaughn (my brother) came and lifted it out for us. (He was not in the pool.) Then as I swam to the other side of the pool, I noticed below me, in the water, Dad was floating with his eyes closed. I dragged him up to the surface and he said, "I was resting in peace." I said, "Well you've rested enough. Time to get out."
Then I woke and feared that the dream means Daddy will soon die.

April 21, 2013
I (dreamed) of Leo last night. (The cousin who died many years ago and appeared in front of the refrigerator to Emily.) We were visiting somewhere – There were others around – I knew them to be with him – We were in his place – not mine. I was ecstatic to be with him! There was sooo much Love. He was as happy to be with me and I was to be with him. The whole area (room) around us was simply ALL LOVE. We were talking – I had been aware all along that we hadn't seen each other for a very long time – but then I realized Leo had died – Quite emotional, I nearly shouted at him, "Are you REAL?"

"Yes, I'm real," he smiled.

"But you died! I remember going to your funeral!" I cried.

"I'm real.," he said, "You just have to believe."

I awoke thinking, "I believe Leo, I believe – and I love you."

The next entry in my dream journal (not a dream) is a big heart with writing inside: Dad's accident was May 31, 2013. He passed on July 06, 2013.

In reading this entry, I believe that in my subconscious, I realized that Leo had come to me to help prepare me for my father's departure. Thank you, Leo. I believe Leo, I believe.

*

In another dream that I had shortly before Dad's accident, I rode in a car, holding a baby girl, with Dad driving. He drove along the river in Frankfort. I became aware that he was going to drive into the river and kill the three of us. Very unlike Dad in real life! I was desperate to stop him, or to at least save the baby in my arms, who I think was my baby sister. But, Dad managed to hold the wheel and the car landed in the river. As it sank, I was absolutely determined to somehow save my sister. But Dad had all the doors and windows locked. We were sinking ...

Now that dream makes more sense to me. Dad did indeed decide to end his life when he refused breathing assist. And it did nearly kill my sister and I who had nursed him tenderly, in the hospital, for five weeks. What saved us was our heartfelt gladness for Daddy's return to God in Heaven.

*

I watched a surfboard like structure bouncing across waves like on a lake. As the board neared my vantage point, I saw my father clearly. He looked about thirty years old. (He had been eighty-seven when he passed.) His auburn hair topped his head in windblown waves. His smile showed his lovely white teeth. Looking directly at me, or at my vantage point – I did not see my own body – he waved. It was a 'So-long,' kind of wave and I knew immediately that my Dad was leaving this dimension and passing into the Kingdom. I was struck by how like him to come see me and let me know, so I wouldn't worry.

*

The month after Daddy died, I was diagnosed with Breast Cancer. One tumor in the left breast and three in the axilla under the left arm. The first treatment was sixteen rounds of brutal chemo. Then surgery and then thirty six rounds of radiation. Lord knows, I was very ill through that chemo treatment. Hospitalized often, I realized I was actually near death. For my sake, I was fine with crossing over. But I knew my husband needed me, so I prayed if it could be my Lord's will, please heal me that I might remain on earth to see my husband through his final years. (He is eleven years older than me and has been through a lot of medical crises.)

Each night, as I lie prone in bed, with my bald head sweating profusely, the leg bone pain kept me tossing and turning. As I lie back after vomiting profusely and losing the content of my bowels all over the place, I felt my Savior's presence. He lay beside me peacefully and offered his arm. His blood, which was a clear golden color, transfused from Him into me – every night – and cleansed my blood of the cancer. After these transfusions, I slept, at least for an hour or two.

During the course of my chemo treatments, when I was probably at my lowest point, I had a dream:

Oct. 23, 2013
Last night's dream:
I walked into a glass atrium of sorts, looking for Mom. There were people scattered in there – not a lot. Plants

4-6 feet tall seemed to grow down the center of the building – just a scattering though – not tightly packed. Down to my far right I saw a woman kneeling in front of the plants – in prayer. I recognized her right away as Aunty Barbara (died about 15 years ago.) She was back to me. I started to back out of the building before she saw me – because I felt I couldn't betray my mother (who disliked Aunty Barbara & Uncle Bob, for most of my life. But then I stopped. I knew that the right thing to do was follow my heart & go see Aunty Barbara. I hoped that my mother would not walk in & see us & be hurt by it – but God's will be done.

I walked up behind Aunty Barbara & said, "Aunty Barbara?"

She got up immediately & turned to me. She smiled so full of love and embraced me. She absolutely infused me with love. "You've got to stay strong," she whispered into my neck.

Without words, she reassured me that I'll make it through this.

To think that I almost missed this important visit, is frightening.

Aunty Barbara would not have forced the meeting on me – It was all up to me. Thank you Aunty Barbara.

As I woke, I realized this was the 2nd time she has come to me in a dream since my diagnosis.

Oh, before the dream ended, Uncle Bob was standing beside Aunty Barbara. He looked me in the eye & said, "I love you." I knew he meant it & it took a lot for him to do that. I was disappointed that I could not tell him that I loved him too. I realized it will take time. He hurt me too badly (over Amy) but I did tell him, "Thank you." It was soft & sincere. We both understood & it was ok. Then he pointed to the sweater vest I wore & smiled to Aunty Barbara, "My sweater vest," (meaning it looked like one he had.) "My Dad's sweater vest," I corrected him. He and Aunty Barbara drifted off with him smiling & talking about the sweater vest.

I would like to mention to the reader that Aunty Barbara and my mother had been in a silent feud for many years, before she passed from cancer. I loved her dearly but knew if I went to speak with her, my mother would be mad. Sure that Aunty Barbara had not seen me, I could have turned around and left without offending her. But, I knew my mother's attitude was wrong. Therefore, I chose to walk down to where the aunt, whom I loved, waited.

During the course of our visit, she offered me two things. First her love was transmitted by the beatific smile she rested on me. Secondly, she impressed upon me four words, "You've got to stay strong." So many doctors, nurses and other folks had given me this advice before; it surely was nothing new to me. But when Aunty Barbara, who had died of cancer, told me this, I listened and I bucked up.

*

Back before my Dad died and before I was diagnosed with breast cancer, I had a dream visit with my cousin Bobby, the son of Aunty Barbara and Uncle Bob. Bobby had passed away when he was only forty-three in 1993. His visit frightened me terribly. He warned me about Emily:

April 14, 2013
Bobby Thibodeau came to me in a dream. He looked fantastic & was very happy. In the dream – I was sitting on a grassy knoll. There were perhaps a couple dozen people milling around, but not near me. It was rural – some trees. I was sitting just meditating – thinking of Bobby & all of a sudden, he just appeared before me – standing up. I looked up at him. He saw how surprised I was. I knew he had died, but it didn't seem unlikely that he could appear & I could see him. He saw my surprise & smiled at me. "What were you just thinking?" He asked me.

"I was thinking about you," I said.

He smiled more broadly. "I think about you a lot," I told him.

"I know," he said.

"But I've been thinking about you a LOT more lately. I miss you."

"I know, I think about you a lot too," he said.

Then he said he had to go buy a tire for Emily. (My daughter.) He explained something about her tire but I can't remember what. I said, "Well I want to pay you for the tire."

"No," he said.

"Yes, I want to," I said.

"Why," he asked.

"Because she's my daughter. She's a dear girl & we don't do much for her."

"No," he repeated.

I asked him, "How do you know Emily?"

Then he explained about something happening on the road & he came along & now he was going to get her a tire. There was more to the dream & Anna was there for part of it, but I just can't remember. (I called Emy this morning & told her about the dream & made her promise to check her tires!) But Bobby somehow let me know, without speaking, that he had saved Emily's life.

It was so good to see him. And he looked the best he ever looked in life! And I was very happy that I felt he loved me too. I was never sure. (Not romantically.) But I always loved him dearly. We had a lot of fun together as kids. And he was Mary's boyfriend in 1st & 2nd grade & his best friend, Stephen Pearson was my boyfriend. ☺

Note to reader:
This dream occurred one month before my father's fatal accident and a little over four months before I was diagnosed with cancer. But outside of these blows to the entire family, Emily's life appeared to be going very well and her tires were fine. How had my visit from Bobby been so far off? I began to doubt my visits and their meanings. But I was certainly grateful that my daughters were flourishing.

Two weeks after I finished my radiation, I received a call from Emily. Could I come to Boston. Her husband, Michael, was hospitalized with pancreatic cancer and would not survive. I went to Boston, not in very good shape, but I was there. Michael died eight days after being diagnosed. Emily's life had completely derailed. But I knew Bobby would be there helping her through.

*

A couple of months after I completed my treatment and surgery, I was at my mother's house. Mom sat in a chair at the kitchen table, back-to to the kitchen door. I had been in the living room and walked towards the kitchen. As I approached the doorway, I saw Nanny enter through the kitchen door. My first impulse was to rush over to her and hug her. Oh, was I ever happy to see her! But no, she had been dead for a long time. I must not be selfish, in this dream visit. I must let Mom see her mother first. So, I stood back and watched as Mom caught sight of her mother. She jumped up and they embraced so joyfully. As they clutched, they rocked and circled there in the kitchen. Then Nanny caught sight of me. She let loose of Mom and glided over to me and we embraced. I felt bad for Mom to have to let go, but I knew by this time, that these ghostly visits from beyond are limited. I knew Nanny would not have much time to spend with us, so I took what I was given. As we held each other, I whispered in her ear, "I suppose you know?"

"Mm," she replied in a non-committal tone.

"They say it might take my life, Nan. Will it?"

"Yes dear," she answered without the least bit of concern. It was just a simple answer. But I was shocked. I had been sure I would beat this thing now that I had completed my treatment.

It has been three years and I'm still here. The cancer may someday, claim my life, as Nanny said. Or perhaps all those prayers have changed the course of history. Our Lord has told us this is possible!

CPSIA information can be obtained
at www.ICGtesting.com
Printed in the USA
BVHW030759250520
580268BV00001B/18

9 781520 636139